L10 R

KU-222-756

Doctor

Margaret Hudson

Contents

Heinemann

Where in the world?

When you are sick you need someone to help you get better. All over the world there are different people who help children to get well and stay well.

We are going to visit four of these people.

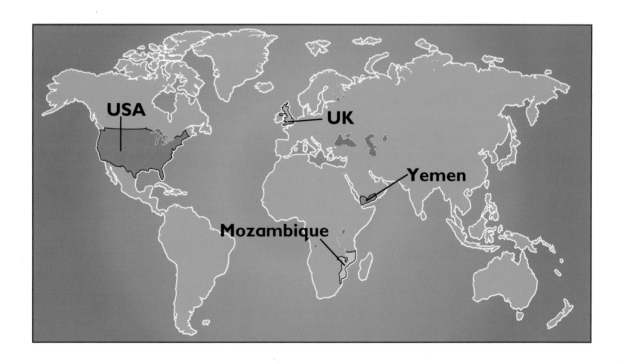

Anne is a **GP** in the countryside in Kent, in the United Kingdom (UK).

Sadia is a **midwife** in the town of Zabid, Yemen.

Dan is a **paediatrician** in the city of San Francisco, in the United States of America (USA).

Inez is a nurse in Macheva, a **suburb** of the city of Maputo, Mozambique.

3

Keeping you well

Different countries have different people to help you keep well.

Anne is a **GP**. She looks after everyone, not just children. She visits some **patients**, like Mrs Heartfield, at home.

Sadia is a **midwife**. She looks after **pregnant** women and their young children. She also teaches other midwives.

Dan is a **paediatrician**. All of his patients are children.

Inez is a nurse. She works in a hospital **clinic**. She looks after mothers and their babies.

United Kingdom

Anne Weatherley lives in a village called Elmstone. The land is very flat. The family ride their bikes a lot. Anne drives to work. Their house is 10 minutes' drive from the **surgery** where Anne works.

Anne sees some **patients** at the
surgery. Three other doctors work at
the surgery too. Nicholas Simon has
come for a **check-up**. Anne checks his
eyes, ears and teeth. She weighs and
measures him too.

Judy Hogben is the **receptionist** at the **surgery**. She answers the phone. She tells people when they can come to see a doctor. She makes a list of people who cannot get to the surgery. Anne visits these people at home.

Anne's husband, Andrew, works too. Their children, Christopher, Jonathan and Katie go to school. They all eat their main meal together in the evening. They are eating minced meat with mashed potatoes on top and vegetables.

Yemen

Sadia and her son live in Zabid with her sister Kabla's family. Sadia's husband is in the army. He is away a lot. Kabla looks after the children while Sadia is at work. Sadia works at the hospital, 10 minutes' walk away.

Sadia sees all her **patients** at the hospital. She is taking a **pregnant** woman's **blood pressure**. Most women in Zabid have their babies at the hospital. Sadia helps to **deliver** many of the babies.

Sadia also looks after the babies when they are born. She weighs and measures them. She checks their eyes, ears and teeth. She talks to their mothers about how to look after them.

Sadia's family eat their main meal in the middle of the day. The six children eat before the adults. They are eating rice, bread, chicken and tomatoes. After that they will eat grapes and bananas.

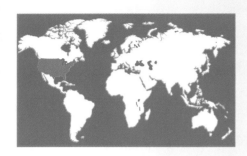

USA

Dan Kelly lives in San Francisco. His wife, Penny, is also a doctor. Their children, Kieran, Devin and Caitlin, all go to local schools. Their house is 20 minutes' drive from Dan's office in the centre of the city.

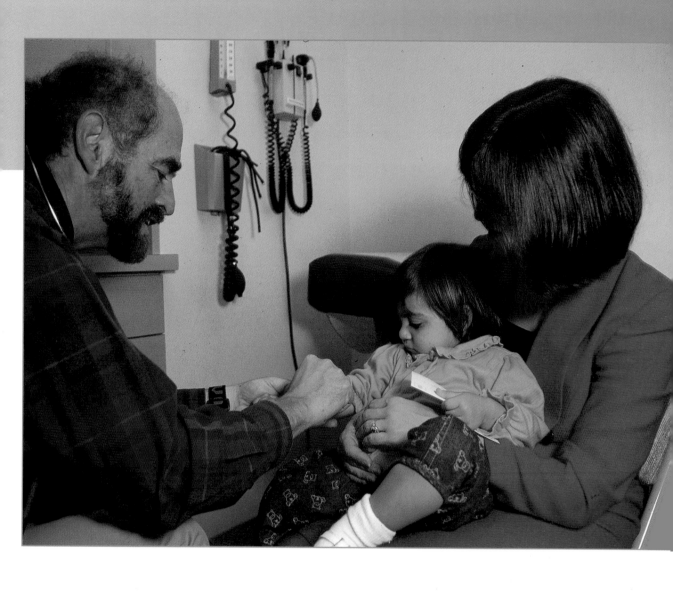

Dan sees all his **patients** at his office. Amalia has come for a **check-up**. She is weighed and measured by a **medical assistant**. Then Dan checks her eyes, ears and teeth. Here he is checking she does not have **TB**. TB is a serious disease, usually found in the lungs.

Dan works with two other doctors. Lisa Woo is a **medical assistant**. She looks after the **patients'** notes and makes **appointments** with patients. She also weighs and measures them before they see the doctor.

The family eat their main meal
together in the evening. They eat a lot
of takeaway food. Dan and Penny
often don't feel like cooking at the end
of a hard day. They are eating a
Chinese meal with noodles, rice, meat
and vegetables.

Mozambique

Inez Jones lives and works in Macheva, a **suburb** of Maputo. She and her four children live with her husband's mother and sister. Her husband is away, working in Johannesburg, South Africa. Inez works in a hospital that is 20 minutes' walk away.

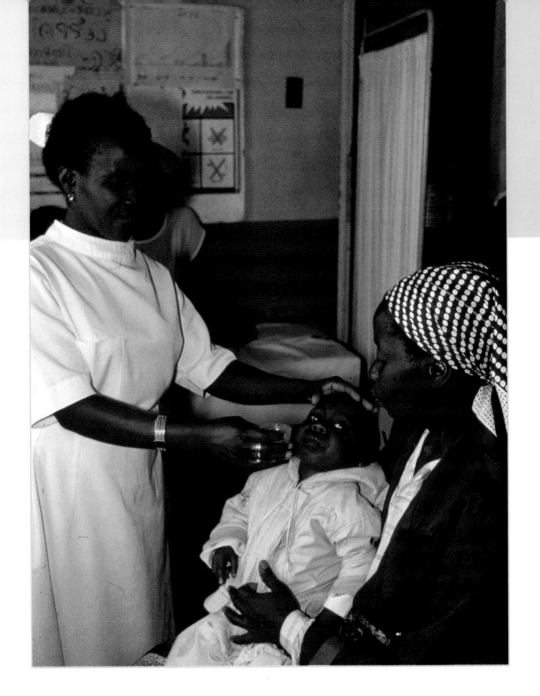

Inez works all morning in the **TB clinic** of the hospital. TB is a big problem in Mozambique. Inez gives **patients check-ups**. She gives medicine to those who need it. She talks to mothers about how to keep their babies healthy.

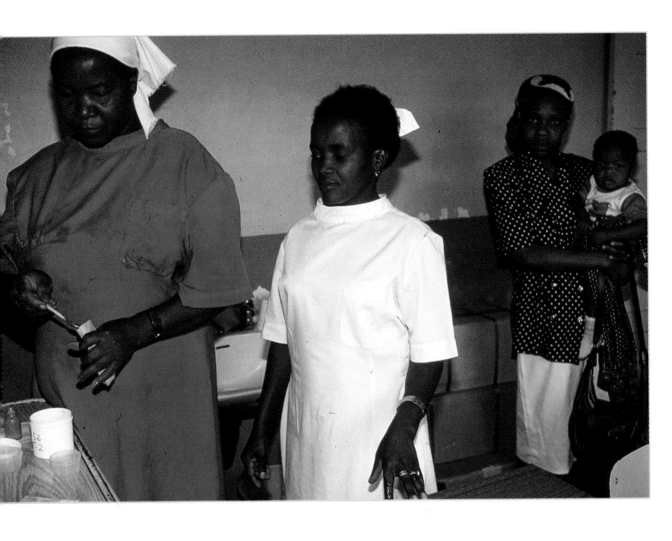

There is a lot of work to do at the **clinic**. Beatrice is Inez's **medical assistant**. She helps Inez to do the work. She mixes some of the medicines and does some of the **check-ups**.

The family eat their main meal in the middle of the day. They are eating pumpkin leaves, rice and beans. Inez's two boys go to school in the city. They eat their main meal with an aunt who lives near the school.

Factfile

Mozambique

Population: 18 million

Capital city: Maputo

United States of America (USA)

Population: 264 million

Capital city: Washington DC

United Kingdom (UK)

Population: 58 million

Capital city: London

Yemen

Population: 15 million

Capital city: Sana

Digging deeper

1 Look at page 3. How are the cities of Zabid, San Francisco and Maputo the same? How are they different?

2 Look at pages 10 and 14. What are the doctor's homes made from? Why do you think they were built like this?

3 Look at pages 7 and 19. Do the doctors work in the same kinds of places?

Glossary

appointments times when patients can see the doctor

blood pressure the force of blood on the walls of the blood vessels. Too much or too little pressure can make you ill.

check-up an examination by a doctor to make sure you are well

clinic a special part of a hospital. Patients who need care but do not need to stay in hospital come here for treatment.

deliver to help a mother to have her baby

GP a general practitioner. This is a doctor who treats all kinds of patients.

medical assistant a helper who looks after medical records and does some checks on patients for the doctor

midwife a doctor or nurse who looks after pregnant women and their babies

paediatrician a doctor who only treats children

patients people who are looked after by medical staff

pregnant going to have a baby

receptionist the person who makes appointments for patients to see the doctor

suburb an area of buildings on the edge of a city

surgery a building where doctors work and see patients

TB (tuberculosis) a disease that can kill you if it is not cured

Index

First published in Great Britain by Heinemann Library
Halley Court, Jordan Hill, Oxford OX2 8EJ
a division of Reed Educational and Professional Publishing Ltd

OXFORD FLORENCE PRAGUE MADRID ATHENS MELBOURNE
AUCKLAND KUALA LUMPUR SINGAPORE TOKYO IBADAN
NAIROBI KAMPALA JOHANNESBURG GABORONE
PORTSMOUTH NH CHICAGO MEXICO CITY SAO PAULO

© Reed Educational and Professional Publishing Ltd 1996

Designed by John Walker

Illustrations by Oxford Illustrators and Visual Image

Printed in Malaysia

00 99 98 97 96

10 9 8 7 6 5 4 3 2 1

ISBN 0 431 06336 2

British Library Cataloguing in Publication Data

Hudson, Margaret
Doctor
1. Physicians – Juvenile literature
I. Title
610.9'2

Acknowledgements

The Publishers would like to thank the following for permission to
reproduce photographs:

Chris Honeywell: pp. 3, 4, 6-9;

Chris Johnson/Oxfam: pp. 3, 4, 10-13;

Jenny Matthews/Oxfam: pp. 1, 3, 5, 18-21;

Sean Sprague: pp. 3, 5, 14-17

Cover photograph reproduced with permission of Jenny
Matthews/Oxfam

Our thanks to Clare Boast for her comments in the preparation
of this book.

Every effort has been made to contact copyright holders of any
material reproduced in this book. Any omissions will be rectified
in subsequent printings if notice is given to the Publisher.

Oxfam believes that all people have basic rights: to earn a living,
to have food, shelter, health care and education. There are nine
Oxfam organizations around the world - they work with poor
people in over 70 countries. Oxfam provides relief in
emergencies, and gives long term support to people who are
working to make life better for themselves and their families.

Oxfam (UK and Ireland) produces a catalogue of resources for
schools and young people. For a copy contact Oxfam, 274
Banbury Road, Oxford, OX2 7DZ (tel. 01865 311311) or contact
your national Oxfam office.

Oxfam UK and Ireland is a Registered Charity number 202918.
Oxfam UK and Ireland is a member of Oxfam International.